breeze-easy method 1

Saxophone

by Valentine Anzalone

Alfred Music
P.O. Box 10003
Van Nuys, CA 91410-0003
alfred.com

ISBN-10: 0-89724-195-9
ISBN-13: 978-0-89724-195-3

Cover Photos Courtesy of C. G. Conn.

FOREWORD

This METHOD offers to the young student a systematic approach to correct concepts in music reading and saxophone playing. The method may be used with equally satisfying results either for private study or for class work. The fundamentals of tone production, technique, rhythmic understanding, and tonal consciousness have been especially emphasized. Additionally, this book offers a refreshing repertoire of new song material that will delight both student and teacher.

Through this course of study in which efficiency and thoroughness have been pin-pointed, the student is guided to take his place as a contributing member of the school band or orchestra in the shortest possible time. Upon completion of books I & II of the "BREEZE EASY" METHOD for SAXOPHONE, the student will be prepared to enter directly into most intermediate saxophone methods.

Valentine C. Anzalone

PLAYING POSITIONS

THE SAXOPHONE IN PLAYING POSITION

THE THUMBS IN PLAYING POSITON

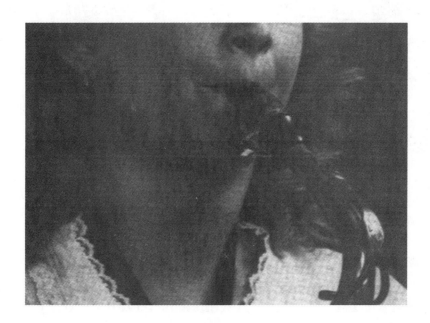

**LIPS & MOUTHPIECE IN CORRECT
PLAYING POSITION**

HOW TO READ THE FINGERING GIVEN
IN THIS BOOK

The Saxophone has 6 buttons which are pointed out and represented by the 6 circles in the fingering diagram below.

This sign — ● — tells us to press the button.

This sign — ○ — tells us not to press the button.

When a key is to be pressed, its number will be given.

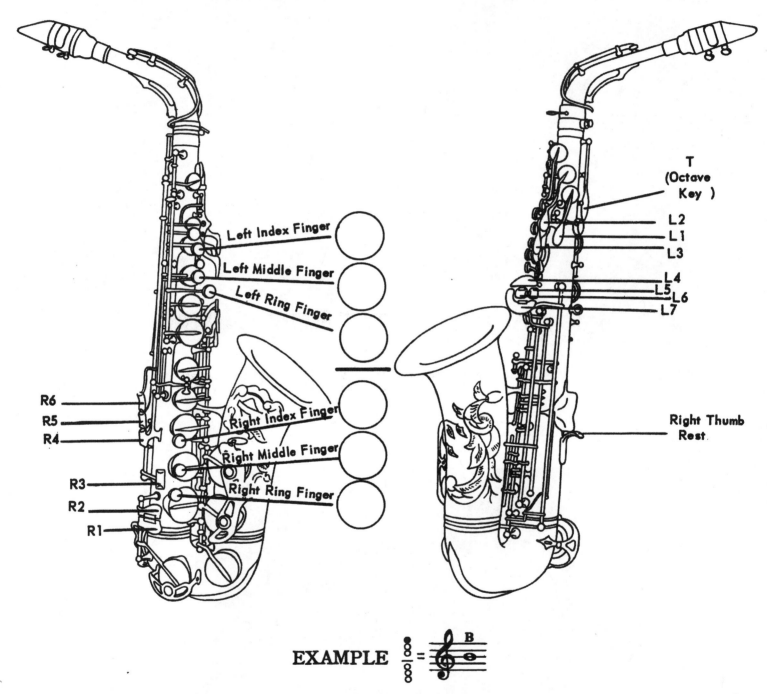

EXAMPLE

The fingering diagram in the example above indicates that you should press only the first finger button with the left index finger.

(A FINGERING CHART for general reference is given on pages 30 and 31.)

PRELIMINARY LESSON

THINGS YOU SHOULD KNOW BEFORE WE BEGIN:

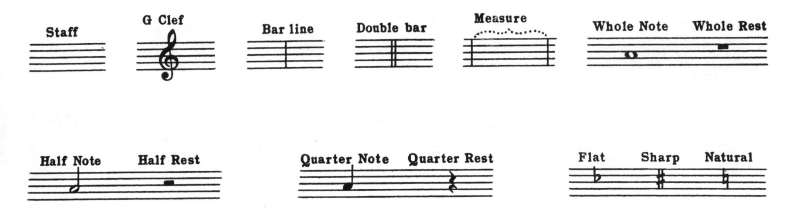

Staff   G Clef   Bar line   Double bar   Measure   Whole Note   Whole Rest

Half Note   Half Rest   Quarter Note   Quarter Rest   Flat   Sharp   Natural

TIME SIGNATURES

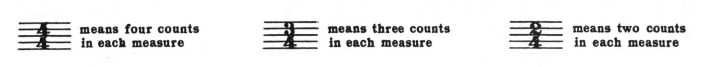

$\frac{4}{4}$ means four counts in each measure $\frac{3}{4}$ means three counts in each measure $\frac{2}{4}$ means two counts in each measure

NAMES OF NOTES

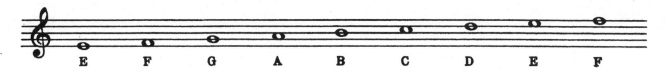

E   F   G   A   B   C   D   E   F

OUR FIRST TONES

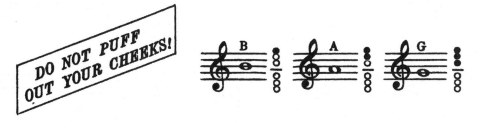

DO NOT PUFF OUT YOUR CHEEKS!

B   A   G

YOUR TEACHER WILL SHOW YOU HOW TO HOLD YOUR INSTRUMENT AND PRODUCE A TONE CORRECTLY. PRACTICE HOLDING EACH OF THE FIRST TONES FOR A LONG WHILE. KEEP TRYING TO IMPROVE YOUR TONE BY LISTENING TO YOURSELF.

(All New Notes and Material will be placed in a box at the beginning of each lesson.)

THIS LESSON HAS BEEN COMPLETED. DATE _____ EXCELLENT ☐ GOOD ☐ FAIR ☐

LESSON 2.

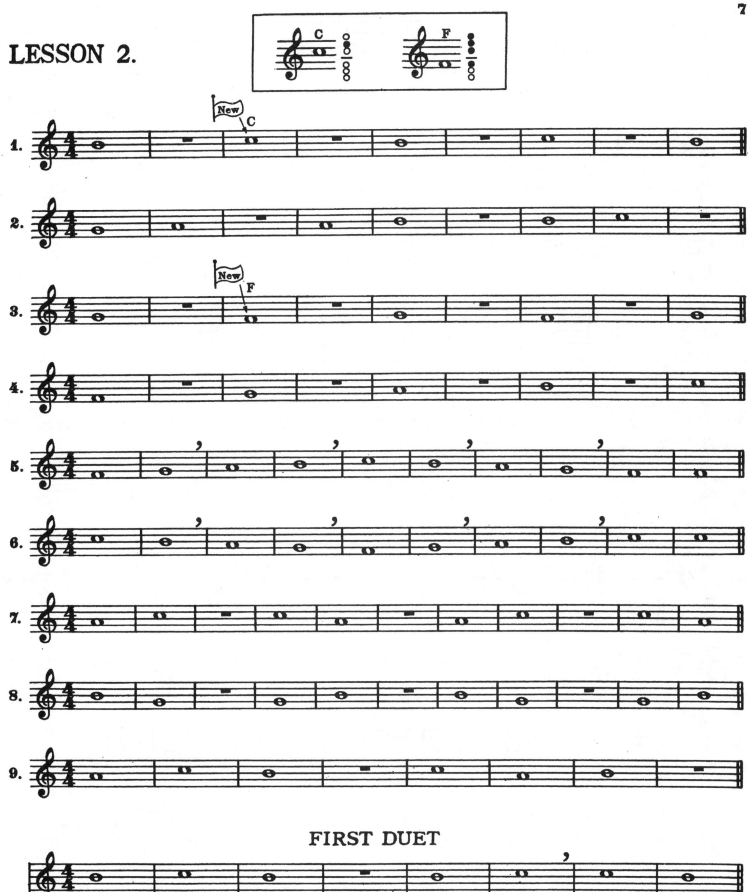

THIS LESSON HAS BEEN COMPLETED.   DATE _____ EXCELLENT ☐ GOOD ☐ FAIR ☐

8

LESSON 3.

| ♩=HALF NOTE | ▬ =HALF REST |

COUNT: 1 2 3 4   1 2   3 4

COUNT: 1 2 3 4

COUNT: 1 2 3 4   1 2 3 4   1 2

SKIPS

HALF NOTE SONG

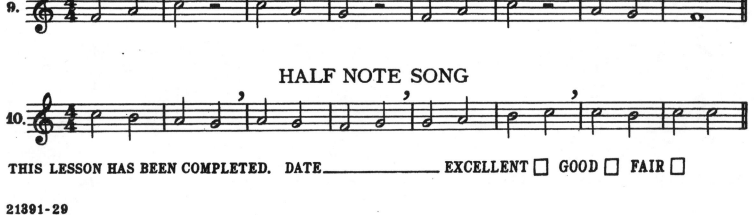

THIS LESSON HAS BEEN COMPLETED. DATE_____ EXCELLENT ☐ GOOD ☐ FAIR ☐

21391-29

LESSON 4. | ♩ = QUARTER NOTE   𝄽 = QUARTER REST |

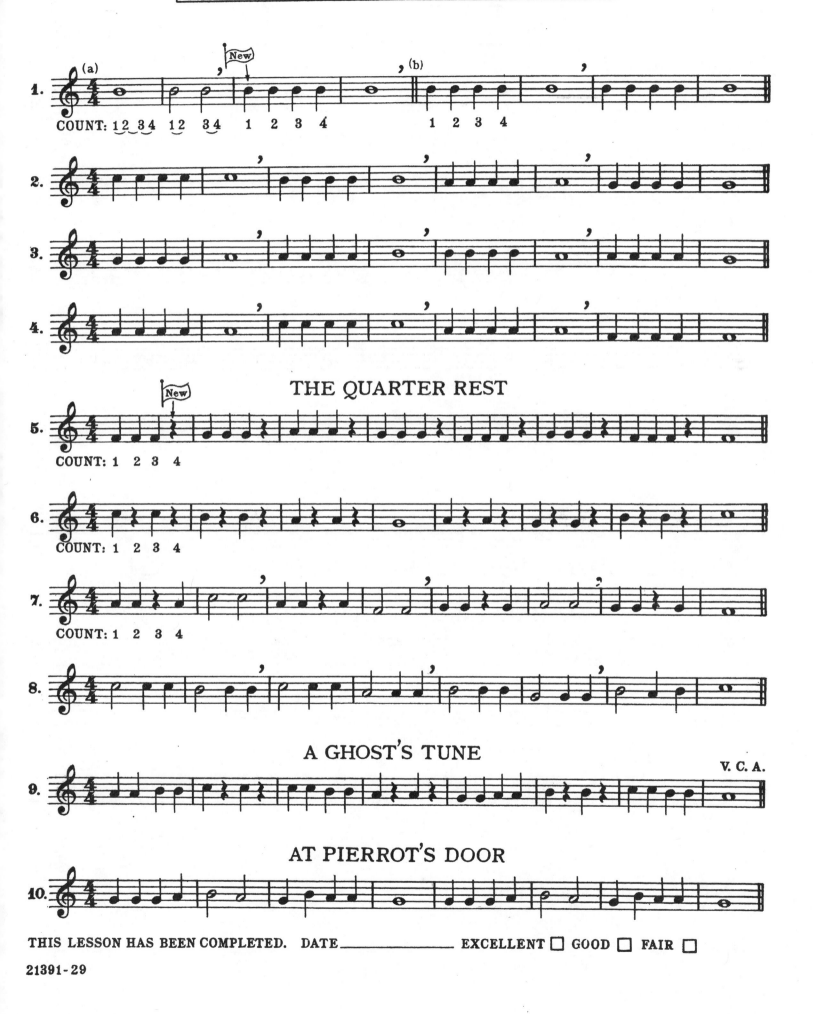

THE QUARTER REST

A GHOST'S TUNE

V. C. A.

AT PIERROT'S DOOR

THIS LESSON HAS BEEN COMPLETED.   DATE_____ EXCELLENT ☐ GOOD ☐ FAIR ☐

21391-29

THIS LESSON HAS BEEN COMPLETED. DATE _____ EXCELLENT ☐ GOOD ☐ FAIR ☐

REVIEW QUIZ NO. 1

THIS LESSON HAS BEEN COMPLETED.   DATE _____   EXCELLENT ☐ GOOD ☐ FAIR ☐

LESSON 7.

HICKORY DICKORY DOCK

LONDON BRIDGE

CHERRIES RIPE

MARCH OF THE KING'S MEN (Duet)

THIS LESSON HAS BEEN COMPLETED. DATE_____ EXCELLENT ☐ GOOD ☐ FAIR ☐

Upon completion of this lesson the student will find much enjoyment in playing from BREEZE-EASY RECITAL PIECES-Book I by JOHN KINYON. This collection of well-known songs has been arranged in the simplest possible fashion and is available with piano accompaniment.

THIS LESSON HAS BEEN COMPLETED.   DATE_____   EXCELLENT ☐ GOOD ☐ FAIR ☐

LESSON 9.

D.C. al Fine = Go back to the beginning and play to *Fine* (End).

SOME HIGHER NOTES

1. add the Thumb key | (add T | (add T | (add T

2. PRACTICE BOTH PARTS

3.

THUMB PRACTICE

4.

5.

GOOD NIGHT LADIES

6.

MARCH FOR SAXOPHONES

7.

New → *Fine (End)*

New → *D.C. al Fine*

THE C SCALE

8.

THIS LESSON HAS BEEN COMPLETED.   DATE_____   EXCELLENT ☐ GOOD ☐ FAIR ☐

21391-29

LESSON 10.

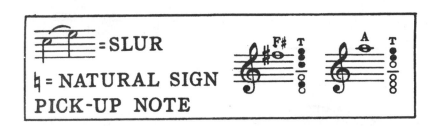

THIS LESSON HAS BEEN COMPLETED. DATE _____ EXCELLENT ☐ GOOD ☐ FAIR ☐

LESSON 11.

THE G SCALE (Memorize)

DUKE STREET

GOING HIGHER

MARCH OF THE VICTORS

V. C. A.

LOVELY EVENING

THIS LESSON HAS BEEN COMPLETED. DATE _____ EXCELLENT ☐ GOOD ☐ FAIR ☐

LESSON 12.

A SINGING GAME

THE C SCALE (Memorize)

CRUSADER'S HYMN

Bb and B♮

ABIDE WITH ME

THIS LESSON HAS BEEN COMPLETED.   DATE _____   EXCELLENT ☐   GOOD ☐   FAIR ☐

LESSON 13.

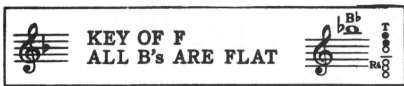

KEY OF F
ALL B's ARE FLAT

HOW CAN I LEAVE THEE

THE F SCALE (Memorize)

CIRCUS WALTZ (Duet)

V. C. A.

Learn both parts

Fine

D.C. al Fine

REVIEW QUIZ NO. 2

The top number in a time sign tells you how many beats are in a measure, for example, in $\frac{3}{4}$ time there are 3 beats in a measure. Fill in the empty measures given below with note values that will be correct for the time sign given.

THIS LESSON HAS BEEN COMPLETED. DATE _____ EXCELLENT ☐ GOOD ☐ FAIR ☐

21891-29

LESSON 14.

♪ ♪ ♫ = EIGHTH NOTES   ⌐ = EIGHTH REST

JINGLE BELLS

THE EIGHTH REST

THE C SCALE

TWINKLE TWINKLE LITTLE STAR

THE BLUE BELLS OF SCOTLAND

THIS LESSON HAS BEEN COMPLETED.   DATE _____   EXCELLENT ☐ GOOD ☐ FAIR ☐

21391-29

LESSON 15.

>= ACCENT MARK

D. S. al Fine - Go back to the sign (𝄋) and play to *Fine* (End).

KEY OF D
ALL F's AND C's ARE SHARP

ACCENT EXERCISE

1.

2.

COUNT: 1 + 2 +

AFTER-BEATS

3.

COUNT: 1 + 2 +

4.

THE D SCALE

5.

GOING HOME (Duet)

DVORAK

6.

POODLES ON PARADE

V. C. A.

7.

(Do not play the 1st ending when going *D. S. al Fine*)

Fine

D. S. al Fine

THIS LESSON HAS BEEN COMPLETED. DATE_____ EXCELLENT ☐ GOOD ☐ FAIR ☐

LESSON 16.

2 = REST 2 CONSECUTIVE MEASURES

THE LONG REST

1.

COUNT: 1 2 3 4 | 2 2 3 4

4 — 1 2 3 4 | 2 2 3 4

3 4 — 1 2 3 4 | 2 2 3 4

TO A WILD ROSE

E. MacDOWELL

2.

THE ERIE CANAL

Traditional

3.

HAPPY LITTLE DONKEY

Traditional Round

4.

FANFARE FOR TWO (Duet)

V. C. A.

5.

THIS LESSON HAS BEEN COMPLETED. DATE _____ EXCELLENT ☐ GOOD ☐ FAIR ☐

LESSON 17.

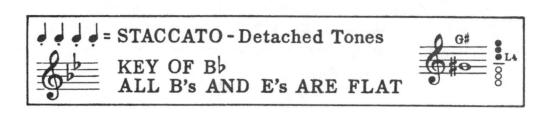

A SCOTCH MELODY

MEASURES 1 & 2 SHOULD SOUND ALIKE BECAUSE OF THE STACCATO MARKS IN MEASURE 2

AMARYLLIS

CHROMATIC SONG

THE B♭ SCALE

FOLK SONG

TECHNICAL EXERCISES

MELODY BY HAYDN

THIS LESSON HAS BEEN COMPLETED. DATE _____ EXCELLENT ☐ GOOD ☐ FAIR ☐

21391-29

LESSON 18.

THIS LESSON HAS BEEN COMPLETED. DATE _____ EXCELLENT ☐ GOOD ☐ FAIR ☐

LESSON 19.

INTRODUCING THE DOTTED QUARTER NOTE

ALMA MATER

PATRIOTIC HYMN

SLURRING PRACTICE

CHROMATIC EXERCISE

O COME ALL YE FAITHFUL

THIS LESSON HAS BEEN COMPLETED. DATE _____ EXCELLENT ☐ GOOD ☐ FAIR ☐

21391-29

LESSON 20.

⅟ = REPEAT SIGN FOR ONE MEASURE

D SCALE AND CHORD PRACTICE (Memorize)

MELODY FROM BEETHOVEN'S 9th SYMPHONY (Duet)

STACCATO EXERCISE

REPEAT THE PRECEDING MEASURE

THE STAR SPANGLED BANNER

THIS LESSON HAS BEEN COMPLETED. DATE_____ EXCELLENT ☐ GOOD ☐ FAIR ☐

21391-29

LESSON 21.

OH! SUSANNA

BLOW THE MAN DOWN

THE MARINES' HYMN (Duet)

THIS LESSON HAS BEEN COMPLETED. DATE_____ EXCELLENT ☐ GOOD ☐ FAIR ☐

LESSON 22.

mf = MEDIUM LOUD	⌢ = HOLD
mp = MEDIUM SOFT	*rit. (ritard.) = slow down*

AULD LANG SYNE

Traditional

New → *mf (medium loud)*

New → HOLD THIS NOTE A LITTLE LONGER

New → *ritard. (slow down)*

f

HYMN OF THANKS

mf

rit.

SONG FOR A DARK RAINY DAY

V. C. A.

New → *mp (medium soft)*

rit.

THIS LESSON HAS BEEN COMPLETED. DATE_____ EXCELLENT ☐ GOOD ☐ FAIR ☐

LESSON 23.

SYNCOPATION

Allegro = Medium Fast
Andante = Medium Slow
Maestoso = Stately

THESE MEASURES ARE PLAYED THE SAME

LIZA JANE

Traditional

mf staccato

NOBODY KNOWS THE TROUBLE I'VE SEEN

Traditional

mf

THEME FROM FINLANDIA

SIBELIUS

CARRY ME BACK TO OLD VIRGINNY

BLAND

mp

Fine

D. S. al Fine

THIS LESSON HAS BEEN COMPLETED. DATE_____ EXCELLENT ☐ GOOD ☐ FAIR ☐

LESSON 24.

crescendo (cresc.) — Gradually Louder
diminuendo (dim.) — Gradually Softer

1.

CHROMATIC EXERCISE

2.

CRESCENDO AND DIMINUENDO

3.

PRAISE FOR PEACE

FLEMING

Andante

4.

THE CHROMATIC SCALE (Memorize)

5.

SHE'LL BE COMIN' ROUND THE MOUNTAIN

Traditional

Allegro

6.

THIS LESSON HAS BEEN COMPLETED. DATE _____ EXCELLENT ☐ GOOD ☐ FAIR ☐

*See Notes Below

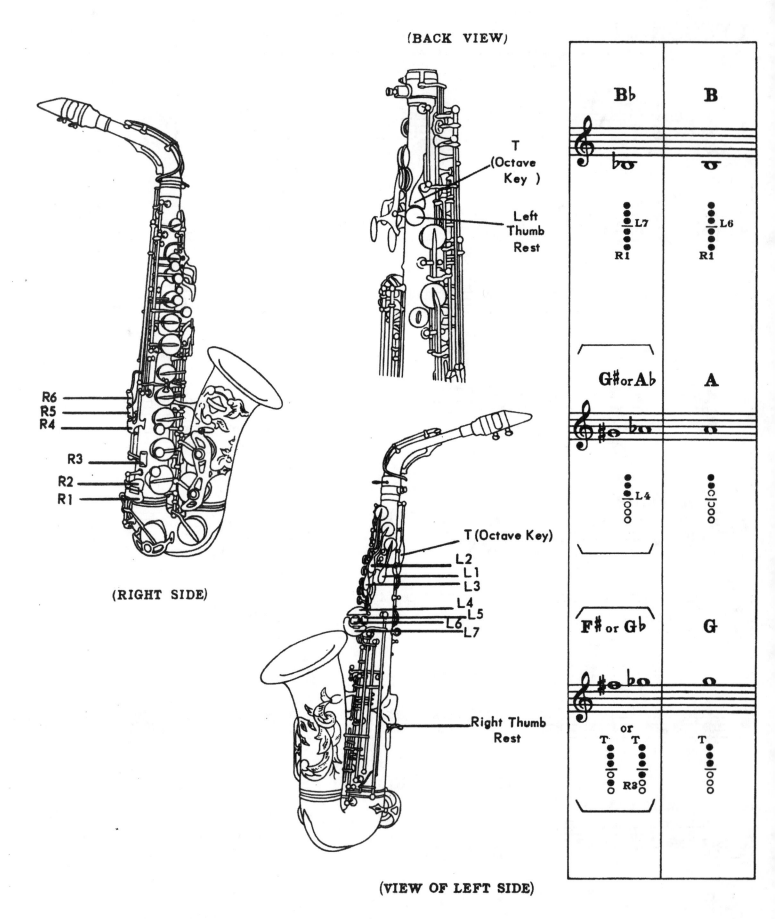

(BACK VIEW)

(RIGHT SIDE)

(VIEW OF LEFT SIDE)

* When two fingerings are given for a note, the one on the left should be learned first.

   Your teacher will tell you when it is best to use the other fingering.

   When two notes are given together (D♯ or E♭), they sound alike and therefore are fingered the same.

FINGERING CHART

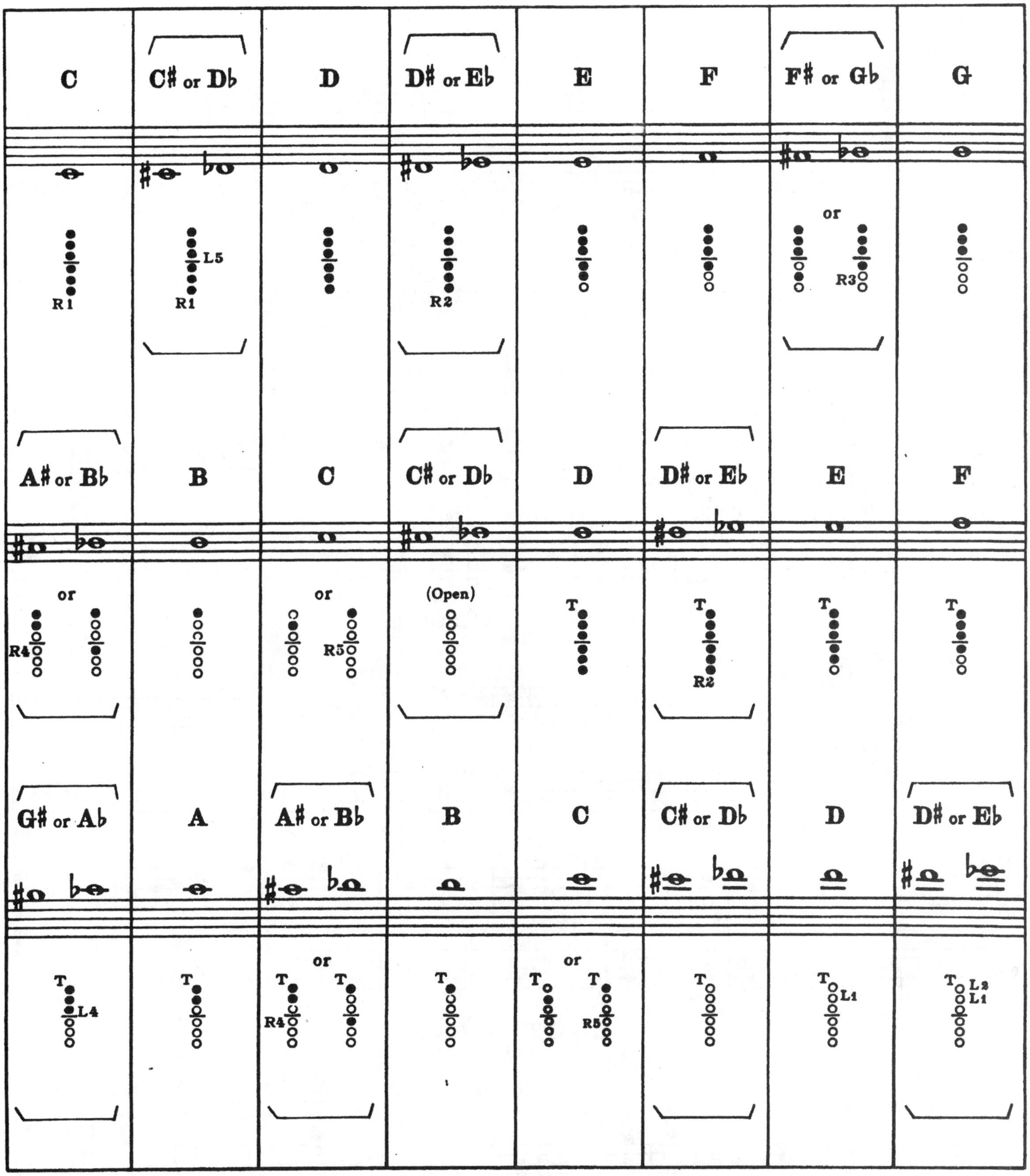

32

The pieces on this page may be played as Solos, Duets, Trios and Rounds as indicated under each title. These Ensembles may be played by groups of "like" or "mixed" instruments (Flutes, Oboes, Trumpets, Drums, etc. may play together). When "mixed" groups play these Ensembles, only F Horns and E♭ Saxophones may be used.

*THE BELL IS RINGING
Round

DOWN BY THE STATION
Round

THE ALPHABET SONG
Duet

MOZART

CLAPPING SONG
Trio

Mexican Folk Song